GALE
CENGAGE Learning

Novels for Students, Volume 3 Copyright Notice

Copyright © 1998

Gale Research
835 Penobscot Building
645 Griswold St.
Detroit, MI 48226-4094

This book is printed on acid-free paper that meets the minimum requirements of American National Standard for Information Sciences—Permanence Paper for Printed Library Materials, ANSI Z39.48-1984.

ISBN 0-7876-2113-7
ISSN 1094-3552

Printed in the United States of America.
10 9 8 7 6 5 4

Cry, the Beloved Country

Alan Paton 1948

Introduction

Alan Paton's novel exploded on the English reading public in 1948. Since then, the society of South Africa has evolved dramatically. Still, Paton's *Cry, the Beloved Country* remains a classic expression of South Africa and one of the best known stories of that country. The implications of the steadfast appeal of the novel are not only a credit to Paton's ability to capture the human tragedy of the Kumalo family, but also testimony to the unfortunate fact that racial tensions still exist both within and without South Africa.

The story itself is about the land of South

Africa and its people as it is expressed in one man's quest to find his son. This mission brings the man, Reverend Stephen Kumalo, to Johannesburg—the great center of the country. Unfortunately, the son, Absalom Kumalo, is found guilty of an awful crime. In the end, the tragedy of Absalom's execution becomes a background for the renewal of the impoverished land. This renewal is made possible by a change in the attitude of a rich white landowner whose son was murdered by Absalom. Alan Paton tells this tale in a simple manner which captures pre-apartheid South Africa in a parable. However, though the tale is one of forgiveness, hope, and learning, there is a feeling of resignation to the misguided policies of what the world would soon know as Apartheid.

Author Biography

Alan Stewart Paton was born in Pietermaritzburg, Natal (now part of South Africa), on January 11, 1903. At the age of twelve, he entered Maritzburg College (a secondary school). After graduating, he enrolled in courses at the University of Natal. While in college he published his first poems in the university's literary magazine. In 1922 he graduated with a degree in physics.

Two years later he held his first political role by representing the students of his alma mater at the first Imperial Conference of Students in London. After this, he taught mathematics and chemistry at Ixopo High School for white children until 1928. That year he joined the staff at Maritzburg College and married Doris Olive Francis. Together they had a son, David Paton, two years later.

In 1935, Paton moved to Johannesburg to serve as principal of Diepkloof Reformatory for African boys. This position was the result of his friend Jan H. Hofmeyr's dual role in the coalition government. Hofmeyr was both head of Education and the Interior. By the power of this position, Hofmeyr transferred juvenile reform from the Department of Prisons to that of Education. Paton, in other words, as an early proponent of racial harmony, was in an ideal position to influence the direction of South Africa. Unfortunately, the hope of a harmonious South Africa lasted only as long as Hofmeyr's reign in government.

One year after becoming principal, Paton joined the South African Institute of Race Relations. He then had another son named Jonathan. When World War II was declared, Paton volunteered but was found ineligible. In 1942, he was appointed to an Anglican Diocesan Commission whose function was to report on church and race in South Africa. In the following year, he authored a series of articles on crime, punishment, and penal reform. In 1944 he addressed the National Social Welfare Conference, and this paper was later published in 1945 as "The Non-European Offender." Then in 1946 he began his tour of penal and correctional institutions in Europe, the United States, and Canada. While on this tour, he began *Cry, the Beloved Country*, published in 1948. At the same time as this novel's publication, Jan Hofmeyr died, and the National Party won the election. Apartheid policies were almost immediately enacted.

The international success of *Cry, The Beloved Country* enabled Paton to be financially independent as well as allowing him to write in opposition to the government and travel abroad. Being known internationally as an author and spokesperson of the conditions in South Africa kept Paton out of trouble with the government. However, the government did confiscate his passport in 1960, not returning it until the early 1970s. In the 1950s he was amongst those who tried to form an opposition Liberal Party to the Nationalist apartheid government. Legislation against non-whites in government forced Paton, who was president of the multi-ethnic party, to disband rather than conform to the new laws in 1968. From his most famous novel of 1948, until his death by throat cancer in 1988, Alan Paton wrote novels, poems, nonfiction articles and biographies, spoke around the world, and remained a proponent of racial equality.

Book I

Cry, the Beloved Country consists of three sections, Books I, II, and III, each presenting a different point of view about the same events. Book I is presented through the eyes of the main character, Stephen Kumalo, a native priest in Ndotsheni, a small community in the Ixopo district of South Africa. The time is 1947. There is a terrible drought that is forcing the young people of the region to leave their agricultural communities and to emigrate to Johannesburg to seek employment in the mines. The loss of so many young people has undermined the tribal traditions, which cannot be maintained in a large urban setting like Johannesburg. The action begins with a letter that comes to Kumalo from Johannesburg, telling him that his sister, Gertrude Kumalo, is ill and needs his help. Kumalo consults with his wife and decides to use their meagre savings to go to the big city to help his sister. His son, Absalom, has also disappeared into the city, and Kumalo hopes to gain word of him as well.

After a long and intimidating journey by train and bus to Johannesburg, Kumalo visits a parish priest named Theophilus Msimangu who helps him to locate his sister. After a long search from one address to another, Gertrude is found living in a shabby room with a young child. She has been working as a prostitute. Kumalo arranges for her and the child to stay with him before they return to Ndotsheni. Kumalo then goes to visit his brother, John Kumalo, who has become a political leader for black rights in Johannesburg. Kumalo's discussions with his brother illustrate the tension between the tribal culture of the past and the new way of living in the city. In the new way of life everyone is on their own with no community, but also without the limitations of living within the rules of the tribe. John Kumalo praises the opportunities available for enterprising people in the city, but Kumalo suggests that his brother John might have protected their sister Gertrude if he had remembered the values of the tribe.

Kumalo then tries to discover the whereabouts of his son, Absalom. As he goes about Johannesburg with Msimangu as his guide, the terrible conditions of the "kaffirs" (native people) are revealed: the overcrowding, the segregation from the white communities where the natives have to work, the lack of transportation, the rising prices and stagnant wages. In fact, the black people have initiated a bus strike to protest a fare hike, and Kumalo and Msimangu must walk many miles in search of Absalom. Sympathetic white people drive up and down the thoroughfares giving the kaffirs rides in their cars in order to support the strike, and Kumalo is greatly impressed by this generosity. Kumalo's search for his son ends at a reformatory where Absalom had been sent after being convicted of theft. The white man who runs the reformatory has released Absalom early for good behavior and found him a job and a place to live. Absalom has a girlfriend with whom he is expecting a child, and he is to marry her soon. Though Kumalo is distressed that his son has broken the law, he is delighted that Absalom seems to be reformed and on his way to living a regular life. The white man and Msimangu lead Kumalo to Absalom's new home so that father and son can be reunited.

When they arrive at Absalom's home they discover that he has abandoned his pregnant girlfriend and resumed his life of crime. The white man is very disillusioned and angry, but Kumalo is grieved at this new evidence of the destruction brought on by the breaking of the tribe. It is discovered that Absalom has been involved in a terrible crime: he and two companions have broken into the home of a white man, Arthur Jarvis, and killed him when the white man surprised them in the middle of the robbery. The irony is that Arthur Jarvis was an important advocate among white men of native rights and was writing a book about how white mistreatment of blacks was the underlying cause of black crime. The magnitude of the crime and its consequences for his family and the black community weigh heavily on Kumalo's mind.

> There is not much talking now. A silence falls upon them all. This is no time to talk of hedges and fields, or the beauties of any country. Sadness and fear and hate, how they well up in the heart and the mind, whenever

one opens the pages of these messengers of doom. Cry for the broken tribe, for the law and custom that is gone. Aye, and cry aloud for the man who is dead, for the woman and children bereaved. Cry, the beloved country, these things are not yet at an end. The sun pours down on the earth, on the lovely land that man cannot enjoy. He only knows the fear of his heart.

Book I ends as Kumalo visits his son in prison. Absalom is remorseful, but has no explanation for his behavior other than the temptations of the city and bad companionship. Kumalo turns for help to Father Vincent, a white Anglican priest who finds an attorney for Absalom, and helps Kumalo through a crisis of faith.

Book II

Book II is presented from the point of view of James Jarvis, the father of the murdered man. Jarvis lives in Ixopo and has a large estate, High Place, near the village of Ndotsheni where Kumalo is the priest. Jarvis is only vaguely aware of the kaffirs and their community, seeing ignorant, dirty people who exhaust and damage their own land with traditional farming techniques. When the news comes that his only child, Arthur, has been murdered in Johannesburg, Jarvis has the sad task of informing his wife and going to the city to stay with his daughter-in-law's family while the body is identified and the estate settled.

While going through Arthur's papers, Jarvis discovers that his son had a great admiration for Abraham Lincoln and believed that Lincoln had much to teach South Africa about race relations. Since Jarvis knew little of his son's opinions about the conditions of the natives, he makes an effort to understand his son's thinking on the race issue. Jarvis reads the Gettysburg Address and Lincoln's second inaugural address, as well as Arthur's writings about the "native question." Jarvis begins to realize that the prejudices he has held against the kaffirs have contributed to the deprivations that natives have suffered in South Africa. He comes to understand that the white ruling class has broken the tribal life of native people by using them as cheap labor in the cities and depriving them of community life by making them live in compounds without their families. Jarvis sees that his son was trying very hard to change the lot of the native majority by giving them a greater share in the benefits and opportunities that the white minority have always enjoyed.

One of Absalom Kumalo's companions in crime is the son of John Kumalo. Though Absalom has determined to tell the truth to the court, John Kumalo advises his son and the other culprit to lie and say they were not there. In spite of the fact that Absalom has the free services of Mr. Carmichael, a white lawyer who defends black clients as a public service, the court condemns Absalom to death by hanging. The two other culprits are acquitted for lack of evidence. Kumalo prepares to return to Ndotsheni to tell his wife the tragic news. When he goes to take Gertrude with him, he finds that she has been lured back into her old life, leaving her son behind. Kumalo returns to his village with the boy and Absalom's pregnant wife. Absalom was permitted to marry her in prison to give their child a name.

Book III

Book III is told from the point of view of both Kumalo and Jarvis, who have returned to their respective homes in Ixopo. Jarvis's grandson, the young son of Arthur Jarvis, makes friends with Kumalo in order to learn to speak Zulu. Because of this relationship, Jarvis learns of the deprivations being suffered in the kaffir village because of the drought. He sends milk to save the dying children, hires an agriculture expert to restore the stricken valley and to teach the people effective farming techniques, and builds a new church in his wife's memory. The two fathers, white and black, become reconciled to one another. Together they represent the hope for South Africa's future.

Mr. Carmichael

Mr. Carmichael is a tall, grave, white man brought to Rev. Kumalo by Father Vincent. He agrees to take up the defense of Absalom "pro deo"—for God, for free. Carmichael agrees to defend Absalom because he is a just man and senses that Absalom is telling the truth but his companions are not. Thus, he tells Kumalo, he could never defend the other two. At once then, Mr. Carmichael is a "godsend" who will do what he can to persuade the court not to execute Absalom. However, he is more than a lawyer, he is a white man who calls Kumalo "Mr. Kumalo" and is all business—no awkward racism. The lawyer is a man of the law, not of nonsense, but still he is unable to get past the paranoia that recent reports of "native" crime has spread amongst the people. The punishment for Absalom is inevitable.

John Harrison

John Harrison is a minor figure who is representative of the "average" white person in Johannesburg. John is the brother of Mary, Arthur Jarvis' wife. As a businessman, he is a part of the white establishment. By association with Arthur, it could be imagined that John is a tolerant person but instead, he says to James Jarvis, "He and I didn't talk much about these things ... I try to treat a native decently ... [but] we're scared stiff." Once, he was asked by a government official to speak to Arthur about toning down his liberal speech. Now, due to the reports of increasing crime and the murder of his brother-in-law, Harrison quite frankly hopes that the police catch Arthur's killers "and string 'em all up."

Arthur Jarvis

Arthur is a white activist who works to further the cause of racial equality in South Africa. His murder, at the hands of Absalom Kumalo, drives much of the action of the novel.

James Jarvis

A white landowner and father of Arthur, Absalom Kumalo's victim. Jarvis's estate is adjacent to the village where Stephen Kumalo lives. The death of his only son hits him hard but does not fill him with vengeance. Instead, he goes to his son's house and reads through his son's papers. There he reflects and accepts his son's thoughts about living as equals among the native peoples. It is not that previously he was a bad man, a miser, or a racist—only that he had been passive and did not do anything to help solve the problems of South Africa. That all changes as he reads the writing of his son and passes this writing to his wife.

When he returns to his estate he begins to

distribute milk for the relief of the children. Then he finds an advisor who will help to restore the barren valley. He does this with the big picture his son presented in his mind. He does this both because it is the right thing to do but also because it will benefit his own family. This later consideration is clearly represented by his grandson who is allowed to ride his horse to the Rev. Kumalo's house for impromptu Zulu lessons.

The fathers meet in a very dramatic moment and both sense the genuine sorrow of the other. One could say they are almost friends, brought together by the tragedy. Yet they are not friends and cannot be. Jarvis is wanting to do right and Stephen is a conduit for that. Stephen in turn can only pray and be a willing conduit—he houses the agricultural advisor, humors the grandson, supports change, and opens his church to Jarvis in the rain. Jarvis, though never an evil man, is the most profoundly changed in the novel. He becomes a crazy liberal rumored to be spending his whole fortune on improvements for the valley. He is a great source of hope to Kumalo and to the reader.

Margaret Jarvis

The mother of Arthur and wife of James Jarvis, Margaret is a representation of motherhood. She shared her son's vision with him when he was alive. His death, and the ensuing change in her husband, serve as the catalyst for her pursuing Arthur's vision. Unfortunately, she is not able to do as much as her husband because her illness worsens. However, her dying wish is that her husband build a new church for St. Mark's Parish where Stephen Kumalo is a minister. The church is built and her memory kept alive by the people of the parish.

Absalom Kumalo

Absalom Kumalo is a product of the changing South Africa. He goes to Johannesburg to find his Aunt Gertrude but instead finds himself with no prospects but mining or crime. He chooses crime more by default and association with others in a similar position. At one point he is in the reform school from which he is let out on account of excellent behavior. The reform authorities hope that he will take the job they arrange for him so he may provide for his young girlfriend who is pregnant. Instead, he abandons the woman he is to marry and goes with two friends into a white neighborhood to steal. The house belongs to Arthur Jarvis, who surprises the three boys and is killed by Absalom.

For this murder Absalom is sentenced to death and finds himself abandoned by his friends. Then he faces his father whom he has shamed. Though by law he must be hanged for his crime, there is a tremendous sense of injustice over the events of which Absalom finds himself the victim. Absalom remains sympathetic to the reader since he acted from fear and did not intend to kill Arthur. Jarvis, unlike Mr. Harrison, does not want Absalom's death for his son's death.

Media Adaptations

- In 1951, Alan Paton and Zoltan Korda produced a film version of *Cry, the Beloved Country* with London Films. Starring Sidney Poitier, the film was recently released on video by Monterey Home Video.

- In 1994, *Cry, the Beloved Country* was recorded on cassette by Blackstone Audio Books.

- In 1995 Miramax filmed a new version of *Cry, the Beloved Country*, starring James Earl Jones and Richard Harris. The film was directed by Darrell James Roodt and produced by Anant Singh.

Gertrude Kumalo

Stephen Kumalo's sister Gertrude left home for Johannesburg in search of her husband who had gone for a job in the mines. Not finding him, she stays in the city and becomes a prostitute. She sells liquor, has a child, and serves time in prison. When she becomes ill, a kindly minister writes to Stephen asking him to come to the city and care for Gertrude. Stephen arrives and removes her to the safety of Mrs. Lithebe's house. In the end, the call of the city is too strong and she slips away, leaving Stephen to care for her son. Gertrude represents the fate of the many "natives" going to the city in the mid-1940s seeking a better life. Unfortunately, most of them are destroyed, irreparably, by the city.

John Kumalo

John Kumalo reveals to his brother Stephen the new morals of the city. This moral code includes leaving his wife, selfishly getting ahead, and believing only in politics because it enables self-gain. John's whole attitude is incomprehensible to Stephen. However, through contact with his brother, representative of this self-seeking code, he learns about anger and betrayal.

Stephen's brother is a politically active man but only because he has the gift of public speech. In fact, John is a self-seeking and corrupt man interested in politics for the power he can gain. John's selfishness is to use the power of his voice to gain respect and power in the community without endangering his carpentry business. He is the voice of the more politically astute men who are organizing the opposition to the government. His son was with Absalom at the murder scene. However, in John's more "worldly" way, he finds a lawyer for his son who enters a not-guilty plea based on denying his presence at the scene. Through this lie, his son is free while his nephew is executed.

Mrs. Kumalo

She is the wife of Stephen Kumalo and mother of Absalom. Her primary function is as a "reality check" on Stephen. As such, she allows the truth of her son's not returning to finish school to be spoken. Having allowed it, the money they were saving for him can now be spent to find Gertrude.

Reverend Stephen Kumalo

Stephen Kumalo is a Zulu clergyman and pastor of St. Mark's Church in a rural district of South Africa. He journeys to Johannesburg because of a letter from Theophilus Msimangu expressing concern over the welfare of Gertrude Kumalo, the clergyman's sister. Concern for her and a verbalization from his wife that his son is not going to return brings Stephen to use the money they had been saving for their son's schooling and go to Johannesburg to find Gertrude and hopefully Absalom. The novel follows his journey to the city, his retrieval of his sister and her son, and the horrifying discovery of his son's crime. Just as he begins to look for his son, he discovers his son has committed murder.

Through Stephen, whose name recalls the martyred saint, the reader can transverse the lines of tension existing in South Africa in the mid-1940s: race relations are deteriorating while nobody wants to admit the reasons why; the land becomes more and more impoverished with the associated problems of hunger and illness among native peoples; society is in upheaval as the culture of the Zulu tribe is dismantled by the economic siren song of the city. Stephen Kumalo, through all this, encounters doubt but then overcomes doubt with hope. He embodies hope, for Africa, for Mr. Jarvis, for the agricultural specialist who has come to help them. This hope, aided by the very generous gift of Msimangu's bank book, dampens the sense of tragedy Kumalo faces all around him.

Kumalo changes throughout the novel because he is subjected to many new experiences. He encounters the city with all its misery, and he gains insight into the effects of segregation on his people. He also sees the efforts being made to better his people. Kumalo is quite surprised by the bus boycott under the direction of Dubula. He is impressed by the organization of the Shanty Town. Then, he encounters within himself some very human passion that he, as a good pastor, did not know. He is angry and almost cruel with the girl that is his son's wife. He is also angry with his brother John. It seems to Kumalo that in the city one cannot be passive nor can one love pastorally or blindly. He brings this back home where he can no longer simply accept the destitution of the people. Fortunately, neither can Jarvis. Stephen Kumalo, then, is on a quest to understand the world, gain peace with it, and create resolution within his own family. None of these goals are met because they each depend on the other and though he might try, Stephen cannot heal South Africa.

Napoleon Letsitsi

Formerly an over-qualified village school teacher, Napoleon Letsitsi is employed by James Jarvis to teach agricultural methods to the people of Kumalo's village. Though employed by a white man, Letsitsi is fervent in his view of himself as working for Africa. He is one of the new generation of blacks (like Dubula and Mandela) who work for equality and whose anthem is *Nkosi Sikelel' iAfrika*. He mirrors the hope Arthur Jarvis wrote about, that South Africa would one day be a harmonious and just society. His role, however, is to see that the land be rejuvenated and, with that process, the people.

Mrs. Lithebe

A widow with a large house, she is wealthy enough not to have to take in boarders. However, Mrs. Lithebe boards Stephen because she thinks it is good to have a priest in the house. She is very kind to him and very sympathetic to his sad tale. She takes in Gertrude, the boy, and the nameless girl on account of Stephen. She does all this because she is a "mother"—a type of person who creates home and hearth for those needing to be nurtured. Again and again she refuses to believe that she is doing anything extraordinary, saying simply, "Why else do we live?" She says this both as a "mother" but also as a symbol of human generosity. That is, she believes that people live to help people.

Reverend Theophilus Msimangu

He is a clergyman at the Mission House in Sophiatown, Johannesburg. A bit of a cynic, Msimangu is extraordinarily compassionate. He offers Stephen reasons for his search and assistance at every step along the way. He is a guide through the city not unlike Virgil who guided Dante through hell in the *Inferno*. And again, like Virgil, he offers explanations for the confusion that Kumalo finds in the city (which itself is set up in a circular pattern not unlike Dante's Hell). For example, Msimangu explains to him the politics of the bus boycott as well as the role of John Kumalo; he opens the eyes of Kumalo to the life that women, like Absalom's girlfriend and Gertrude, lead; he also has a wider understanding of the change occurring in South Africa—an understanding not unlike that of Arthur Jarvis. At the end, he has decided to give up all worldly goods and withdraw to an ascetic life. In doing so, he gives Stephen his life savings. This money not only happily replenishes all that Stephen had to use for the journey, but puts Stephen ahead.

Msimangu, as a guide, is humble, generous, and wise. He is not unbelievably good because, as he admits, God touched him and that's all. At each stage of Stephen's search he handles details, gains information, and leads him to the next stage. He brings him to trial and supports him throughout. Then, with the gift of the money, he is gone from the story though remembered in the prayers of Stephen.

Father Vincent

Father Vincent is a jolly Anglican priest from England who warmly befriends Stephen at the Sophiatown Mission House. Being a foreigner, Father Vincent portrays the European who is sympathetic to the plight of South Africa. He helps Stephen out with prayer and diverts his thoughts onto the beauty of the land. They discuss South Africa and Vincent tells Stephen about England. When Stephen finds his son in prison and sees that he needs a lawyer, he asks Father Vincent for help. Father Vincent goes to the best lawyer for the job— Mr. Carmichael.

Nature and Its Meaning

The tone of the novel, set from the first paragraph, is like a parable told of a distant place of beauty. Yet within that idyllic setting something is going horribly wrong. By the end of the second paragraph, the tone has changed to show that nature's lush greenness is actually fragile and interdependent with humans. "Destroy it and man is destroyed." *Cry, the Beloved County* is first and foremost the story of a land exploited and left to suffer by a people running after gold. Paton's story contains hope that a balance can be regained by raising awareness about the state of things so that the "natives" will have hope and men like Jarvis will make concessions so as to help them help themselves. It is a hope that the children will not care so much for ownership of the land or things, but for the beauty of the land and for each other.

From the start of Stephen Kumalo's journey to retrieve his family from Johannesburg, there is the unsettling presence of the land. Some critics have said that the land itself is a character in the novel whose pit of illness is the city. First, the land is described as lovely grass and hills, but then attention is drawn to the jarring effect of the road cutting through them. Next, as Kumalo journeys towards the city, the scars of industry are more pervasive as are the burdens on his people. Finally, the city is all noise and pollution and people. Africa is a sick person needing rescue from all those who depend upon it. Like Gertrude, the ill sister Stephen searches for, Africa is calling for someone to rejuvenate it. However, though Jarvis begins by sending an expert, Mr. Letsitsi, the reader can only hope that the land will have more success than Gertrude.

Clearly, the land's health or illness is isomorphic, that is having similar appearance, to the healthy state of the tribe and the nation. The land is the only concern of the tribal leader since most of his people have left for the city. The land is a common conversational topic amongst black and white farmers who are concerned at the growing length of time between rains. There is something very wrong in Africa, and people feel it. The land is ill and society seems to be out of order with itself. Unfortunately, the people decide to worsen things by increasing the burden on the majority of its population—the non-whites—and by doing little to restore the vitality of the withering beauty of the land.

Fear

Fear, the emotion that never seems to diminish throughout the novel, is ever present to Stephen. He fears for the land, for his son, for Jarvis, for all he sees in the city. Everyday a new fear arises and the greatest is that his faith is somehow pointless. This fear is a very important element at a crucial juncture in the novel. At the Mission House they have all just heard the news report of Arthur's death, but it is yet unknown who the culprit is. A sense of foreboding descends and Kumalo says privately to Msimangu, "Here in my heart there is nothing but fear...." Here Paton clev erly broadens the scope of this fear to include people generally.

Chapter twelve opens, "Have no doubt it is fear in the land," and the reader is allowed to know this because Paton provides bits of conversations of white people. The whites fear the blacks, and Kumalo fears that his son may be the one who killed Arthur Jarvis, thus setting off the most recent wave of hysterical paranoia in the city. Then there is the obvious fear of the white man's law and the impossibility of Absalom escaping death.

At the end of the novel, Paton lays all his cards on the table. Through Kumalo he suggests that the only reason Africa is not happy and healthy is fear. It is because people, white and black, are afraid of Kumalo and his wife, the young demonstrator, and Msimangu—afraid that such people would walk upright in the land, might be "free to use the fruits of the land," might sing *Nkosi Sikeleli' iAfrika*, God bless Africa.

Race and Racism

James Jarvis allows the reader the best insight into race relations in South Africa when he reads his son's work. In contrast to Arthur's sensitive theories is the more general outcry over the crime of Absalom. Arthur gives a reason for both the poor state of race relations and general hysteria. In the manuscript Arthur was working on at the time of the crime, Jarvis reads, "The truth is that our civilization is not Christian; it is a tragic compound of great ideal and fearful practice, of high assurance and desperate anxiety, of loving charity and fearful clutching of possessions." In other words, Arthur felt that it was the inaction of able people like himself that allowed South Africa to deteriorate to its present state. Arthur's suggested solution, one that Mr. Letsitsi would appreciate, was the creation of the South African. Indeed, Arthur felt that the biggest problem was that the English bore English, the Afrikaners more Afrikaners, and the natives were general labor. To get around this, a unified South Africa would have to be created. Mr. Letsitsi, on the other side, was working for Africa too—thus he sang the yet little known an-them *Nkosi Sikelel' iAfrika.*

The political rhetoric and the newspapers are not so logical or sober as the writings of Arthur Jarvis. Instead, as the pressure on the state increases due to the migration of blacks from the broken tribes to the city, the whites call for more separation and more exploitation. An effect of this pressure is visible in the hysterical pronouncements made in response to Absalom's crime in chapter twelve. People call for absolute separation by the division of Africa into white and black areas. Others call for the stricter enforcement of pass laws. Well-meaning whites seek to provide more money for education in hopes that this will give blacks more positive goals, thus preventing future crimes. However, none cry for integration, none call for the difficult investigations into the causes of South Africa's woes. Such causes, as Arthur hints, are too deep to be easy. Consequent to these calls, the political party favoring more separation was gaining adherents. In this way, the book prophesied the victory of the National Party. In fact, all throughout the book, the majority of whites are not like Arthur or his father but like Mr. Harrison, who sees the natives as "savage" and not as people with complex personalities and problems like the struggling Kumalo, the intelligent Msimangu, or the motherly Mrs. Lithebe.

Topics for Further Study

- Research the system of apartheid. Find out what the system meant legally as well as culturally and then

try to find out the justifications, moral and ethical, for its existence. In what ways was it like Jim Crowism in the American South? In what ways did it differ?

- Watch *Cry Freedom* and compare it to *Cry, the Beloved Country*. Among other similarities, consider to what extent both works are examples of a white sympathizer exploiting black oppression or how they celebrate the role of the white outsider to raise awareness of the downtrodden other.

- Research the international politics of 1948, especially any tensions between the United Nations' Declaration of Human Rights and the installation of Apartheid in South Africa.

- In the last sections of the novel there is a great deal of concern about the environment. Research the problems caused by population displacement and refugee migration in Africa. What is the condition of the environment in South Africa today? Has the land been replenished or has the situation worsened?

- Find out what is going on in South Africa today and consider the place of Paton's novel now that Apartheid has been dismantled.

Style

Point of View

Paton tells his story as if from a dream. The opening, "There is," implies the story is happening right now, though it is not. The use of the present tense makes the story seem distant, yet possible. The story is a third person narrative. The narrator, however, is not omniscient (all-knowing)—only giving necessary information or as much as would be known in the situation. That is, readers do not ever know a great deal about any of the characters, only how they behave given the plot of the story. The words used to tell this story are reminiscent of Biblical language. The prose is simple and intermixed with religious intonations and references. This is due both to the main characters being Anglican clergymen but also because South Africa, as a Christian nation, might best understand itself represented in a parable fashion. Taking this into account adds even more significance to the comments of Arthur Jarvis as well as the overall complex self-reflection of the novel. The novel is aware of itself as novel—as a story being told far from Africa about the affairs of Africa. This distance is also important to the point of view; it may be third person but it is also written far away from the scenes that the author describes. *Cry, the Beloved Country* was popular, in fact, abroad before it was even known at home.

Dialect

The diction of the novel is influenced by the Zulu and Xosa tongues—not surprisingly as the novel takes place amongst members of those peoples colonized by speakers of the English language. Curious phrases from those languages are rendered into English to sound beautiful yet medieval. For example, women who are mature are greeted as "mother"; at parting they say, "go well, stay well" or just "stay well." Today, this choice of prose style sounds oldfashioned. Then again, some critics of the 1940s remarked that Paton was a bit too oldfashioned and sentimental for their taste. Another example of native-influenced syntax is the way simple words are used and repeated: "This thing, he said. This thing. Here in my heart there is nothing but fear. Fear, fear, fear." Such adoption of local dialect is also symptomatic of the author's effort to capture emotion. To capture emotion in words effectively demands simplicity, repetition, and terse exchanges between characters. Thus, rather than come off as patronizing, Paton accomplished emotional density by staying simple and adopting local phrases.

Apostrophe, Aphorism, and Parallelism

Paton's writing has much in common with the style typical of Hebrew poetry. For this reason, *Cry, the Beloved Country* was often said to be quasi-Biblical. Three rhetorical devices found both in the

Bible and in Paton's novel are apostrophe, aphorism, and parallelism. For an example of the apostrophe, one need go only so far as the title, taken from a passage within the text. This technique involves the direct address of the inanimate for sympathy or aid. The passage which gives us the title begins, "Cry, the beloved country for the unborn child." That is, the country is being asked to have mercy on the future.

The second device is aphorism. An aphorism is the use of a wise saying. This technique is employed often in the speech of Msimangu. For example, "It suited the white man to break the tribe … but it has not suited him to build something in the place of what is broken." Or again, "It is fear that rules this land." Msimangu is authoritatively pronouncing a wisdom he has discovered through careful reflection.

The third technique occurs when Msimangu gives a sermon in chapter thirteen and the narrator attempts to describe his incredible voice. The narrator does this by a parallelism wherein an object (in this case, Msimangu's voice) is related to many things instead of being defined: "For the voice was of gold, and the voice had love for the words it was reading. The voice shook and beat and trembled, not as the voice of an old man shakes and beats and trembles, but as a deep hollow bell when struck…." Parallelism links descriptive phrases in a series so as to compound the complexity and amplify the impression of the object being described. With these serial phrases, the narrator embellishes the power of the voice by hypothesizing what else the voice does or what else the voice is like. The voice is related to things which the reader already knows to be valuable like "gold" and "love." Due to the associations, the reader imagines that he or she has arrived at the idea of the voice's magnificence independent of the help of the narrator but simultaneously with Kumalo.

Dramatic Irony

Dramatic irony is a moment of high drama that occurs when at least one character is lacking information known to the reader. Paton employs this technique expertly in chapter twenty-five when, by chance, Kumalo and Jarvis meet. Jarvis has no idea who the black clergyman is. The two fathers meet at Barbara Smith's on a day when the court is not in session. Kumalo is looking for Sibeko's daughter who was rumored to have worked there. It is on this errand for Sibeko that Stephen finds the father of his son's victim. Jarvis, however, sees only a poor, old, black clergyman. For the reader, as for Stephen, this is a highly charged encounter precisely because one of the participants is unaware of the identity of the other.

Post-World War II

Though World War II had been over for several years, the war was still in the minds of people all over the globe in 1948. The economies of nations directly involved in the war were still recovering and the United States Congress voted for the implementation of the 1947 Marshall Plan to help rebuild Europe. Meanwhile, the Soviet Union and the United States were beginning what Bernard Baruch, advisor to President Truman, called the "Cold War." The first action of this war began where World War II ended. Soviet forces blockaded access to Berlin on June 24, 1948. In a non-violent act to ignore the blockade, the United States and Britain countered with a great airlift of 4,500 tons of food and necessities per day until the Soviets allowed normal transit to return on September 30, 1949. At home, this "cold war" fueled political suspicion by the formation of the "Un-American Activities Committee." This committee was formed to investigate anyone who had Communist affiliations. The most famous 1948 case before this committee involved Alger Hiss. The case is still controversial today though Hiss is dead and Moscow has said he was never a spy.

As the two superpowers began their arms race, the colonies of the British empire began to struggle for independence. India struggled free with the help of Mahatma Gandhi, who was once a resident and prisoner of South Africa. In 1948, Gandhi was assassinated by those resentful of his allowance of partition with Pakistan. Other newly independent nations included Burma and Israel.

Apartheid in South Africa

South Africa was formed in 1910 when the former British colonies of Natal and the Cape joined with the republics of Transvaal and the Orange Free State. It was at this time that the descendants of early Dutch speaking settlers began to refer to themselves as Afrikaners, their dialect as Afrikaans, and their party as the Afrikaner Nationalists. Yet another force in South Africa in 1910 was the African population that outnumbered the whites, were still largely tribal in their political makeup, and lived in rural communities. However, a population shift was occurring that mirrored population shifts everywhere—away from the traditional rural community to the city. In South Africa, due to the dramatic expansions of mining and industry in general, that meant a shift to Johannesburg. This large city was built upon the mining fields where gold had been discovered in 1886.

The Afrikaner Nationalists ruled South Africa from 1924 until 1939. In that year, the liberal agenda of men like Jan H. Hofmeyr took over and people began to have hope that South Africa would be a more equitable and just society. World War II began and South Africa fought on the side of the Allies against the Germans. After the war there was an even greater influx of Africans into the cities and into Johannesburg. It is at the post-World War II moment that Alan Paton sets his novel *Cry, The Beloved Country.* As that novel showed, there were two sides to South Africa in 1945. On one side were the Africans struggling to carve out a living in shanty towns or in rural areas whose soil was depleted. White men like Arthur Jarvis were awakening to the problems that inequality had created and joined with other whites to do what was possible to improve the situation of the natives. On the other side, the influx of people and the increase in crime in the city created a degree of paranoia amongst the enfranchised citizens. Thus in the election year of 1948, after the death of Hofmeyr, the Afrikaner Nationalists were voted back to power because they promised to restore order.

In 1948, the Afrikaner Nationalists began a system of government called apartheid. This system was similar in many ways to Jim Crow discrimination policies in America against African Americans. However, one very important difference was that it was a national policy legally discriminating on the basis of race. Under this system native Africans lived in designated areas and were required to carry "passes" and identity papers on them at all times. The inability to provide an enquiring official with one's papers meant jail or fines. These passes said where the individual could go. Generally, the system of apartheid aimed to keep the nonwhite people living under South African rule a disciplined pool of workers. Thus they did not tolerate dissent or organization into labor unions or political parties. They did so by imprisoning men like Nelson Mandela and Steven Biko for crimes against the state. Recently, Nelson Mandela was released from prison, resumed his political place as head of the African National Congress, and was elected President of South Africa. In 1996, he signed a new constitution for the Republic of South Africa.

Compare & Contrast

- **1948:** Winning the national election, the National Party institutes a system of apartheid, officially segregating the black majority from the white minority.

  Today: Nelson Mandela, having served twenty-seven years in prison, is sworn in as the President of South Africa in 1994. In 1996 he signs the new Constitution which, among other things, guarantees equal treatment before the law for all citizens —black or white.

- **1948:** Those in opposition to Apartheid policies take hope in a brighter future by singing *Nkosi Sikelel' iAfrika.*

Today: The anthem of hope, *Nkosi Sikelel' iAfrika*, has become the national anthem of South Africa.

- **1948:** The British Empire is crumbling as former colonies declare independence.

  Today: The Soviet Union has collapsed and its republics have declared independence.

Critical Overview

The critical reputation of *Cry, the Beloved Country* in the international community has been overwhelmingly positive. Alan Paton's novel, both written and submitted to publishers while on a tour, received much praise the moment it was released. It sold out on its first day of appearance and entered its sixth print run by the end of the year. Back home in South Africa, however, the newly independent Paton was not so warmly embraced. The novel was critical of the new regime and Afrikaners because of their narrow vision and fear-ridden pride. Conversely, black South Africans could never forgive Paton for being a white and could never see the book as anything but a parable written by a white man—sympathetic though he was. The most positive reviewer from this camp was Dennis Brutus, a poet who was a prison inmate with Nelson Mandela. Brutus attributed a new sort of writing in South Africa to Paton and his novel. Paton, said Brutus, set in motion a writing that viewed apartheid critically in such a way as to move people and awaken them to our blight of inhumanity. Unfortunately, Brutus's valuation was retrospective as well as a minority opinion. Martin Tucker, in his book *Africa in Modern Literature*, said that few writers were indebted to Paton. Even so, *Cry, the Beloved Country* outsold all other books except the Bible in South Africa.

Though the first print run was small, the critics

picked up the novel and sounded its triumph. The *New York Times Review*, the *New York Herald Tribune Weekly Book Review*, and the *Yale Review* were all enthusiastic in 1948 when the novel was released. They applauded the new sense of lyricism which Paton had brought English literature by the adoption of the Zulu and Xosa syntax. They praised the breadth of the subject matter yet simple style of the book. While still positive, there were those critics who seemed to miss the point of the novel. One example was Harold C. Gardiner's review in which he says, "the story is preeminently one of individuals. There are no sweeping and grandiose statements about 'the race problem.'" Apparently, he would have preferred a normal protest novel to the more poetic parable Paton wrote.

In 1957, Sheridan Baker wrote an interpretive article which found that the geography of Paton's story was not only symbolic but that it was the same type of Christian allegory to be found in Bunyan's *The Pilgrim's Progress* and Dante's *Divine Comedy*. This would not have been so bad, says Edward Callahan in his 1991 book, but Baker used his idea about Paton's work in an educational packet wherein children were instructed by Baker to make ludicrous associations in the novel. Fortunately, the article by Harry A. Gailey entitled "Sheridan Baker's 'Paton's Beloved Country,'" in which Gailey says that the interpretation of Baker is textually baseless, is also included in the anthology of Baker.

A more rational approach to the novel was close by. Edmund Fuller wrote glowingly of the novel in his *Man in Modern Fiction.* There he wrote that *Cry, the Beloved Country* "is a great and dramatic novel because Alan Paton, in addition to his skill of workmanship sees with clear eyes both good and evil, differentiates them, pitches them in conflict with each other, and takes sides." Thus, while moving only slightly beyond the obvious praise for Paton's political stance, a critic was seeing the story as that of an individual quest for meaning and not just a political protest.

Most criticism of the book simply sides with Paton due to the political tension of the work. In fact, there is little variation amongst the reviewers when it comes to what it is in the novel which deserves praise. Mostly, it was felt that the quasi-Biblical language of the novel was an emotional catalyst that helped to place the reader on the side of the Kumalos and only secondarily with the Jarvis family. Typical of these reviews is that by Edwin Bruell in "Keen Scalpel on Racial Ills." In that article he compared Paton's novel with Harper Lee's *To Kill a Mockingbird* because both novels present children as the innocent victims of society's molding forces. Another review by Myron Matlaw in *Arcadia* simply sums up the critical view of Paton: "Understatement, deceptive simplicity, repetition, selectivity of narrative, episode, and setting, as well as the emotional charge of Paton's style—all these are manifested in Paton's characters as well."

In a recent book by Edward Callan, *Cry, the Beloved Country: A Novel of South Africa*, the view is taken that the book is a classic because of its endurance. After forty years and two movies, Paton's novel is still widely read. He also cites the work as having a universal appeal because of its poetic language and its theme of human responsibility. The setting for the novel, adds Callan, has changed incredibly in that span of time but he makes no prediction about how this will affect the reception of the work.

Sources

Sheridan Baker, "Paton's Beloved Country and the Morality of Geography," in *College English*, Vol. 19, November, 1957, pp. 56-61.

Edwin Bruell, "Keen Scalpel on Racial Ills," in *English Journal*, Vol. 53, December, 1964, pp. 658-61.

Edward Callan, *Cry, The Beloved Country: A Novel of South Africa*, Twayne, 1991.

Edmund Fuller, *Man in Modern Fiction: Some Minority Opinions on Contemporary American Writing*, Random House, 1958, p. 40.

Harry A. Gailey, "Sheridan Baker's 'Paton's Beloved Country,'" in *College English*, Vol. 20, December 1958, pp. 143-44.

Harold C. Gardiner, *In All Conscience: Reflections on Books and Culture*, Hanover House, 1959, pp. 108-12.

Myron Matlaw, review of *Cry, the Beloved Country* in *Arcadia*, Vol. 10, No. 3, 1975.

Martin Tucker, *Africa in Modern Literature: A Survey of Contemporary Writing in English*, Ungar, 1967.

For Further Study

Graham Hough, "Doomed," in *London Review of Books*, December 3-16, 1981, pp. 16-17.

> Rather than praise the novel for its political place, this critic restates the reason for this novel being viewed as a classic: it is the story of an individual grappling to understand the complexity of life in a society so obviously unjust as a racist one.

Tom McGurk, "Paton's Nightmare Came True," in *New Statesman*, Vol. 115, No. 2977, April 15, 1988, pp. 7-8.

> Written when things looked their worst in South Africa, McGurk feels that Paton's novel foreshadowed the increased racial oppression under Apartheid. He also tells the story of Paton's work being taught in school although he does not see this as the hopeful glimmer it will eventually prove to be.

William Minter, "Moderate to a Fault?" in *New York Times Book Review*, November 20, 1988, p. 36.

> In this article, Minter examines the concept of justice in Paton's novels and in his personal life.

Herbert Mitgang, "Alan Paton, Author and Apartheid Foe, Dies of Cancer at 85," in *New York Times*, April 12, 1988, pp. A1, D35.

> In this obituary, Mitgang chronicles the achievements of Paton's life as a writer, teacher, and political leader.

CPSIA information can be obtained
at www.ICGtesting.com
Printed in the USA
LVHW050901140122
708387LV00014B/1183